Language Lessons *for* Children

by Kathy Weitz

Primer Two Winter
Student Book

Acknowledgements

Although my name is on the cover, the Primer series in many ways has been a collaborative effort. I owe a great debt of gratitude to many folks. The gorgeous cover designs are the craftsmanship of my friend Jayme Metzgar, with image credit to The Graphics Fairy (www.thegraphicsfairy.com). Many other friends have helped with both editing and content: in particular, Kimberlynn Curles, Emily Cook, Cheryl Turner, Karen Gill, Carolyn Vance, Lene Jaqua and the exceptional teachers, moms, and students of Providence Preparatory Academy. And of course, the main source of help and encouragement in myriad ways—from design consultation to field testing to dinner duty—has come from my dear husband and my wonderful children.

~kpw

© Copyright 2014. Kathy Weitz
Cottage Press
www.cottagepress.net

Printed in the United States of America.

All rights reserved. This book or any portion thereof may not be reproduced or used in any manner whatsoever without the express written permission of the publisher except for the use of brief quotations in a book review.

Primer Two Winter
CONTENTS

Materials Needed for Primer Two Winter vi

Week 1 3
When Mother Reads Aloud
Rhyming Words
Noun Review
Possessive Nouns & Pronouns
Homonyms, Synonyms, & Antonyms

Week 2 13
from Prince Caspian
Verbs Expressing Action
Verbs Expressing Being or State
*Spelling Rule: Silent **e** With a Soft **c** or **g***
Personification

Week 3 23
from Job 38
Verb Tense: Present, Past & Future
Noun Review
Possessives
Verb Review
Correct Use of Verbs: Loose & Lose
Homonyms, Synonyms, & Antonyms

Week 4 33
from Pinocchio
Singular & Plural Verbs
Suffixes: Two-Syllable Base Words
Verb Review
Homonyms, Synonyms, & Antonyms
*Spelling Rule: **i** Before **e***

Week 5 43

Stopping By Woods

Subjects & Predicates
Rhyming Words
Subjects & Predicates
Personification & Onomatopoeia

Week 6 53

A Laconic Answer

Correct Use of Words: Shall & Will
Suffixes: Base Word Ending in Silent e
Subjects & Predicates
Writing a Friendly letter
Derivatives
Homonyms, Synonyms, & Antonyms

Week 7 63

Our God, Our Help In Ages Past

Verb Tense: Past, Present, & Future
Rhyming Words
Subjects & Predicates
Writing a Friendly letter
Onomatopoeia & Simile

Week 8 73

from The Children's Book of Birds

Conjunctions
Noun Review
The Business Letter
Subjects & Predicates
Homonyms, Synonyms, & Antonyms

Week 9 83

from The Wind

Pronouns & Personification
Rhyming Words
Subjects & Predicates
The Business Letter
Nouns & Pronoun Review

Week 10 93

from Heidi

Questions & Word Order
Suffixes: Changing **y** *to* **i**
Subjects & Predicates
The Business Letter
Homonyms, Synonyms, & Antonyms

Week 11 103

All Glory, Laud, and Honor

Conjunctions & Commas
Rhyming Words
Subjects & Predicates
Noun Review
Homonyms, Synonyms, & Antonyms

Week 12 113

The Good Samaritan

Conjunctions & Commas
Suffixes: Review
Homonyms, Synonyms, & Antonyms

Appendix... 123

The Parts of A Friendly Letter
The Envelope
United States Postal Abbreviations
The Business Letter

Materials Needed for Primer Two Winter

All materials, resources, and links listed below are available at Cottage Press:

www.cottagepress.net

Required

- ❧ PRIMER TWO TEACHING HELPS ~ Required to effectively teach all lessons in in Primer. This one book contains teaching helps for all three Primer One student books. It contains instructions for all nature study and picture study lessons, tips and notes for teaching the Spelling, Grammar, and Word Usage lessons, and an answer key for the exercises that warrant it. Teach each lesson in Primer with this book open for ready reference.

- ❧ PRIMER RESOURCES WEBPAGE ~ Linked from *cottagepress.net* with many resources for nature and picture study. Bookmark this webpage.

- ❧ PICTURE STUDY PDFS ~ Free, downloadable PDFs for individual artists that include images of selected paintings along with biographical notes and links to many online resources. Available artists include: Audubon, Bruegel, Cassatt, DaVinci, Delacroix, Durer, Homer, Michelangelo, Millet, Monet, Rembrandt, Renoir, Rubens, Stuart, Titian, Van Eyck, Van Gogh, Vermeer. The *Primer Resources Webpage* has links to these free PDFs.

- ❧ THIRTY MORE FAMOUS STORIES BY JAMES BALDWIN ~ This is a timeless collection of short narratives that every student should know from history and literature. All narration selections for *Primer Two Winter* are found in this book. Purchase this from the Cottage Press bookstore or download it for free from Project Gutenberg.

  www.mainlesson.com

- ❧ HOME GEOGRAPHY FOR PRIMARY GRADES BY C.C. LONG ~ This book is used for several nature lessons in each of the *Primer Two* books. Purchase this from the Cottage Press bookstore or download it for free from Project Gutenberg.

  www.gutenberg.org/ebooks/12228

- ❧ A SYSTEMATIC PHONICS AND SPELLING PROGRAM ~ The lessons in the *Primer* books are designed to reinforce phonics and spelling rules taught in such a program. See recommendations on the *Primer Resources Webpage*.

OPTIONAL
- HIGH QUALITY COLORED PENCILS ~ Prismacolors by Berol are wonderful!
- BOOKS AND RESOURCES FOR THE NATURE AND PICTURE STUDY LESSONS ~ Links to resources (both free and for purchase) are available on the *Primer Resources Webpage*. Check your local library also. *Webpage*. Check your local library also.

Weekly Lessons

When Mother Reads Aloud

When Mother reads aloud, the past
    Seems real as every day;
I hear the tramp of armies vast,
I see the spears and lances cast,
    I join the thrilling fray;
Brave knights and ladies fair and proud
I meet when Mother reads aloud.

When Mother reads aloud, far lands
    Seem very near and true;
I cross the deserts' gleaming sands,
Or hunt the jungle's prowling bands,
    Or sail the ocean blue.
Far heights, whose peaks the cold mists shroud,
I scale, when Mother reads aloud.

When Mother reads aloud, I long
    For noble deeds to do —
To help the right, redress the wrong;
It seems so easy to be strong,
    So simple to be true.
Oh, thick and fast the visions crowd
My eyes, when Mother reads aloud.

~ Author Unknown

Week 1 • Day 1

Today is _____
                    Day   Date   Year

Columbus and The Egg
~ Thirty More Famous Stories Retold by James Baldwin

Vocabulary to study before you read:

voyage	scholars	foolish
trial	inhabited	hailed
anxious	respect	pauper
conceited	experiment	upright

Draw a picture or series of pictures illustrating the story.

Week 1 ♦ Day 1

Copybook

Copy the title and first stanza from this week's copybook selection into your copybook. Check your work, word by word, against the original.

Did you

❑ include every word in the original and spell every word correctly?
❑ capitalize every letter that is capitalized in the originall?
❑ include every punctuation mark in the original?

Rhyming Words

Each stanza of this hymn has a set of three rhyming words at the end of the first, third, and fourth lines. Each stanza also has a pair of rhyming words at the end of the second and fifth lines, and one more pair at the end of the sixth and seventh lines.

Write the rhyming sets or pairs from this week's poem with endings that are spelled the same.

_____

_____

_____

_____

Write the rhyming words from the poem with endings that are spelled differently.

_____

_____

*Write several words that rhyme with **spear**. Try to write at least two with an ending that is spelled differently.*

_____

Week 1 • Day 2

Today is _____
                    Day   Date   Year

Nature Study

Read The Moon *(found in* Teaching Helps*).*

For the next month, keep track of the shape of the moon. Check at least every two or three nights, and draw the shape of the moon on a calendar in your Nature Notebook.

Sketch the phases of the moon in the frames below.

New Moon	**Waxing Crescent**	**First Quarter**
Waxing Gibbous	**Full Moon**	**Waning Gibbous**
Last Quarter	**Waning Crescent**	**New Moon**

Nature Notebook: Draw, color, and label the phases of the moon. Construct your blank calendar pages and begin recording the shape of the moon each night.

Week 1 • Day 2

Copybook

Copy the second stanza from this week's copybook selection into your copybook. Check your work, word by word, against the original.

Did you

❑ include every word in the original and spell every word correctly?
❑ capitalize every letter that is capitalized in the originall?
❑ include every punctuation mark in the original?

Noun Review

From this week's copybook selection:

Write three nouns that name persons. Tell whether each is common or proper.

_____

Write six nouns that name places.

_____

_____

Write three common nouns that name things or ideas.

_____

For each of the singular nouns, write the plural form; for each of the plural nouns, write the singular form.

| day | armies | lances |

_____

| knights | ladies | eye |

_____

7

Week 1 ♦ Day 3

Today is _____
         Day   Date   Year

Read And Narrate

Upon a Peak in Darien I
~ *Thirty More Famous Stories Retold* by James Baldwin

Vocabulary to study before you read:

isthmus	islets	rappings
provisions	doublet	embroidered
dashing	overbearing	astonished
impassable	loftiest	exultation
merely	oppress	pitch

Draw a picture or series of pictures illustrating the story.

Week 1 • Day 3

Copybook

Copy the third stanza and the attribution from this week's copybook selection into your copybook. Check your work, word by word, against the original.

Did you

- ☐ include every word in the original and spell every word correctly?
- ☐ capitalize every letter that is capitalized in the originall?
- ☐ include every punctuation mark in the original?

Possessive Nouns & Pronouns

An apostrophe (') + s is added to a noun to show ownership. To form the possessive of plural words ending in -s, add the apostrophe (') alone

    John's hat, leaves' flight

Write the correct possessive forms. Include the thing possessed.

tramps of armies   _____

lance of a knight   _____

peaks of heights   _____

waves of an ocean   _____

Write an original sentence with one of the possessives you made.

_____

_____

Two nouns and one pronoun in this week's copybook selection are possessive. Write them along with the things possessed:

_____

Week 1 • Day 4

Today is _____
                        Day   Date   Year

Picture Study

In the space above, make your own rendering of the current work of art using colored pencils, or paste a printout from the Picture Study PDF. Write the title and date of the work on one line, and artist's name below it.

Week 1 • Day 4

Dictation

Homonyms, Synonyms, & Antonyms

Write:

a homonym for past _____

a homonym for real _____

a synonym for vast _____

an antonym for brave _____

a synonym for scale _____

an antonym for simple _____

Write an original sentence using the homonyms you wrote above.

Drawing Page

from PRINCE CASPIAN

It was long and steep, but when they came out on the roof of the tower and Caspian had got his breath, he felt that it had been well worth it. On his left was the gleam of the Great River, and everything was so quiet that he could hear the sound of the waterfall at Beaversdam, a mile away. There was no difficulty in picking out the two stars they had come to see. They hung rather low in the southern sky, almost as bright as two little moons and very close together.

"Are they going to have a collision?" he asked in an awestruck voice.

"Nay, dear Prince," said the Doctor (and he too spoke in a whisper). "The great lords of the upper sky know the steps of their dance too well for that. Look well upon them. Their meeting is fortunate and means some great good for the sad realm of Narnia. Tarva, the Lord of Victory, salutes Alambil, the Lady of Peace. They are just coming to their nearest."

"It's a pity that tree gets in the way," said Caspian. "We'd really see better from the West Tower, though it is not so high."

Doctor Cornelius said nothing for about two minutes, but stood still with his eyes fixed on Tarva and Alambil. Then he drew a deep breath and turned to Caspian.

"There," he said. "You have seen what no man now alive has seen, nor will see again."

~ C.S. Lewis

Week 2 • Day 1

Today is _____
                Day   Date   Year

Upon a Peak in Darien II
~ *Thirty More Famous Stories Retold* by James Baldwin

Vocabulary to study before you read:

ravine	gaunt	clamber
gnarled	verdure	faint
aroused	laden	waylay
obliged	provinces	traversed
exploits		

Draw a picture or series of pictures illustrating the story.

Week 2 • Day 1

COPYBOOK

Copy the title and first paragraph from this week's copybook selection into your copybook. Check your work, word by word, against the original.

Did you

- ☐ include every word in the original and spell every word correctly?
- ☐ capitalize every letter that is capitalized in the originall?
- ☐ include every punctuation mark in the original?

VERBS EXPRESSING ACTION

Study these sentences, taken from this week's copybook selection.

The two stars *hung* low in the southern sky.

Doctor Cornelius *stood* still.

The word hung *expresses the* **action** *of the two stars. The word* stood *expresses the* **action** *of Doctor Cornelius. A word that expresses* **action** *is called a* **verb**.

Find the sentences in the copybook selection with a similar thought to each of these sentences. Fill in the blank with the appropriate verb expressing action:

They _____ out onto the roof of the tower.

Doctor Cornelius _____ in a whisper.

The stars _____ their dance well.

The doctor _____ a deep breath and _____ to Caspian.

Some words that express action can be used as either nouns or verbs. Look at these sentences:

The river *gleamed* in the moonlight. The river's *gleam* caught his eye.

In the first sentence, the verb gleam *expresses the action of the river. In the second sentence, the noun* gleam *does the action of catching his eye.*

Challenge: There are several other words in this week's copybook selection that could be used either as nouns or as verbs. Look for these, and discuss them with your teacher.

Week 2 • Day 2

Today is _____
            Day   Date   Year

Nature Study

Read The Constellations *(found in* Teaching Helps*).*

This week, go outside one clear night and observe the stars. Look at the way they are grouped. Sketch what you see in the box below. Can you make patterns from what you have drawn?

Nature Notebook: On another clear night this week, go outside and draw the stars that you see. Place a compass rose in the correct orientation on your drawing. Also, remember to keep up your moon phases calendar.

COPYBOOK

Copy the second and third paragraphs from this week's copybook selection into your copybook. Check your work, word by word, against the original.

Did you

- ❑ include every word in the original and spell every word correctly?
- ❑ capitalize every letter that is capitalized in the originall?
- ❑ include every punctuation mark in the original?

VERBS EXPRESSING BEING OR STATE

Some verbs do not express action.

Caspian *is* the true prince.

The climb *was* long and steep.

In the first sentence, the word is expresses Caspian's **being**—*who or what he is. In the second sentence, the word was expresses the climb's* **state**—*its condition. A verb is a word that expresses* **action**, **state**, *or* **being**.

Find the sentences in the copybook selection with a similar thought to each of these sentences. For each sentence, supply the appropriate verb expressing being or state:

The gleam of the Great River _____ on his left.

Everything _____ so quiet.

Their meeting _____ fortunate.

Sometimes verbs are made up of more than one word.

They *had come* to see two stars. They *will be coming* to see two stars.

Find the sentences in the copybook selection with a similar thought to these sentences. Supply each missing verb made up of two words.

You _____ _____ what no man now alive _____ _____, nor _____ _____ again.

Week 2 • Day 3

Today is _____
                     Day   Date   Year

READ AND NARRATE

Fountain of Youth
~ *Thirty More Famous Stories Retold* by James Baldwin

Vocabulary to study before you read:

distinguished	appointed	abounding
undertaking	stanch	harassed
kindled	inquiries	limpid
fell	lingered	bewailing

Draw a picture or series of pictures illustrating the story.

Copybook

Copy the fourth, fifth, and sixth paragraphs and the attribution from this week's copybook selection into your copybook. Check your work, word by word, against the original.

Did you

❑ include every word in the original and spell every word correctly?
❑ capitalize every letter that is capitalized in the originall?
❑ include every punctuation mark in the original?

Spelling Rule: Silent E With a Soft C or G

Words ending in the soft sound of c or g very often have a silent e. Do you remember why this is so? The letter c always says /s/ before e, i, or y. The letter g may say /j/ before e, i, or y. A silent e after the c or the g indicates that the c or the g makes its soft sound.

Words that end with a silent e drop the e when adding a suffix that begins with a vowel, unless dropping the e interferes with some other rule. If dropping the silent e would change the sound or the soft the c or g, the silent e must remain.

Add the indicated suffixes to these words. Discuss with your teacher why the silent e is either dropped or kept in each word.

dance + -ing	dance + -er	dance + -ed
peace + -ful	peace + -able	courage + -ous
change + -ing	change + -ed	change + -able
force + -ing	force + -ed	force + -ful

Week 2 • Day 4

Today is _____
          Day   Date   Year

Picture Study _____

Dictation

Personification

Consider these sentences from this week's copybook selection:

    The great lords of the upper sky know the steps of their dance too well.

    Tarva, the Lord of Victory, salutes Alambil, the Lady of Peace.

*Do stars literally dance? No, they cannot; they do not even have feet. Do they literally salute one another? No, they cannot; they do not even have hands. But the author uses these words to bring the scene vividly before our eyes. He **personifies** the stars, comparing them to lords and ladies who dance together and salute one another.*

*There are two ways that an author can create **personification**:*

- ✓ Inanimate objects are given qualities or actions of living things
- ✓ Non-humans are given human characteristics or actions

Look and listen for personification in your reading, and even in your everyday speech. Here a few more examples. Discuss the personification in each with your teacher.

    The frost painted a picture on my window.

    The wind whispered through the trees.

    The wise old owl sat on an oak.

Drawing Page

from Job 38

"Where were you when I laid the foundations of the earth?
    Tell Me, if you have understanding.
    Who determined its measurements?
    Surely you know!
    Or who stretched the line upon it?
    To what were its foundations fastened?
    Or who laid its cornerstone,
    When the morning stars sang together,
    And all the sons of God shouted for joy?"

"Can you bind the cluster of the Pleiades,
    Or loose the belt of Orion?
    Can you bring out Mazzaroth in its season?
    Or can you guide the Great Bear with its cubs?
    Do you know the ordinances of the heavens?
    Can you set their dominion over the earth?"

    ~ Job 38: 4-7, 31-33, New King James Version

Week 3 • Day 1

Today is _____
         Day   Date   Year

"Eureka!"
~ *Thirty More Famous Stories Retold* by James Baldwin

Vocabulary to study before you read:

fashion	grain	wrought
examined	workmanship	puzzled
quantity	displace	bulk

Draw a picture or series of pictures illustrating the story.

H

Copybook

Copy the title and first four lines from this week's copybook selection into your copybook. Check your work, word by word, against the original.

Did you

- ❏ include every word in the original and spell every word correctly?
- ❏ capitalize every letter that is capitalized in the originall?
- ❏ include every punctuation mark in the original?

Verb Tense: Present, Past & Future

A verb is a word that expresses **action**, **state**, *or* **being**. *The* **tense** *of a verb tells* **the time** *when the action, state, or being occurred.*

The sons of God *shout* **for joy. The sons of God** *shouted* **for joy. The sons of God** *will shout* **for joy.**

In the first sentence, the verb shout *indicates that the action is happening at the* **present** *time. In the second sentence, the verb* shouted *indicates that the action happened in the* **past**. *In the third sentence, the verb* will shout *indicates that the action will happen in the future. The simple verb* **tenses** *are* **present**, **past**, *and* **future**.

Rewrite each of these sentences twice: a) Change the underlined verb to simple past tense. b) Change the underlined verb to simple future tense by adding will *in front of the verb. In the second sentence, you also need to change the form of the verb* are.

The morning stars sing together.

Past _____

Future _____

The Pleiades are in the night sky.

Past _____

Future _____

Week 3 • Day 2

Today is _____
　　　　　　　　Day　　　　　　　　　　Date　　　　　　　　　　Year

Nature Study

Read Ursa Major *and* The Big Dipper *(found in* Teaching Helps*).*

Sketch a picture of **Ursa Major** *and the* **Big Dipper** *contained within it. Try to observe it in the night sky this week.*

Nature Notebook: Were you able to see the Ursa Major in the night sky this week? If so, draw it from your own observation. Place a compass rose in the correct orientation on your drawing. Also, remember to keep up your moon phases calendar.

Week 3 • Day 2

Copybook

Copy the middle five lines from this week's copybook selection into your copybook. Check your work, word by word, against the original.

Did you

    ❑ include every word in the original and spell every word correctly?
    ❑ capitalize every letter that is capitalized in the originall?
    ❑ include every punctuation mark in the original?

Noun Review

From this week's copybook selection:

Write three proper nouns that name constellations.

_____

Write three common nouns that name ideas.

_____

Write three common nouns that name places or things.

_____

Possessives

Write the alternate possessive forms. Include the thing possessed.

earth's foundations _____

cornerstone of it _____

belt of Orion _____

ordinances of heavens _____

Week 3 • Day 3

Today is _____
                     Day   Date   Year

Read And Narrate

Galileo and the Lamps
~ Thirty More Famous Stories Retold by James Baldwin

Vocabulary to study before you read:

invented	discoveries	cathedral
pendulums	vibrated	phenomenon
various	timepieces	inquiring

Draw a picture or series of pictures illustrating the story.

Week 3 • Day 3

Copybook

Copy the final six lines and the attribution from this week's copybook selection into your copybook. Check your work, word by word, against the original.

Did you

- ☐ include every word in the original and spell every word correctly?
- ☐ capitalize every letter that is capitalized in the originall?
- ☐ include every punctuation mark in the original?

Verb Review

Rewrite each of these sentences twice: a) Change the underlined verb to simple past tense. b) Change the underlined verb to simple future tense by adding will *to the verb. Change the form of the verb if needed.*

I <u>guide</u> the Great Bear with its cubs.

Past _____

Future _____

Earth's cornerstones <u>are fastened</u>.

Past _____

Future _____

Correct Use of Verbs: Loose & Lose

The verb loose *means to unleash something or let it go. The verb* lose *means to misplace something or fail to keep it. Write two short sentences, demonstrating the proper use of* loose *as the verb in one and* lose *as the verb in the other.*

Week 3 • Day 4

Today is _____
             Day   Date   Year

Picture Study _____

Week 3 • Day 4

Dictation

_____

_____

_____

_____

_____

_____

Homonyms, Synonyms, & Antonyms

Write:

a homonym for laid   _____

a homonym for its   _____

a synonym for ordinances   _____

an antonym for shouted   _____

a synonym for dominion   _____

an antonym for fastened   _____

Write an original sentence using the synonyms you wrote above.

_____

_____

Drawing Page

from Pinocchio

How it happened that Mastro Cherry, carpenter, found a piece of wood that wept and laughed like a child.

Centuries ago there lived—

"A king!" my little readers will say immediately.

No, children, you are mistaken. Once upon a time there was a piece of wood. It was not an expensive piece of wood. Far from it. Just a common block of firewood, one of those thick, solid logs that are put on the fire in winter to make cold rooms cozy and warm.

I do not know how this really happened, yet the fact remains that one fine day this piece of wood found itself in the shop of an old carpenter. His real name was Mastro Antonio, but everyone called him Mastro Cherry, for the tip of his nose was so round and red and shiny that it looked like a ripe cherry.

As soon as he saw that piece of wood, Mastro Cherry was filled with joy. Rubbing his hands together happily, he mumbled half to himself:

"This has come in the nick of time. I shall use it to make the leg of a table."

~ Carlo Collodi

Week 4 • Day 1

Today is _____
                      Day   Date   Year

Sir Isaac Newton
~ *Thirty More Famous Stories Retold* by James Baldwin

Vocabulary to study before you read:

amused	unexplored	ignorant
satisfied	reasoned	draws
matter	contains	surface
force	gravitation	proper

Draw a picture or series of pictures illustrating the story.

Week 4 • Day 1

Copybook

Copy the title and first four paragraphs from this week's copybook selection into your copybook. Check your work, word by word, against the original.

Did you

- ☐ include every word in the original and spell every word correctly?
- ☐ capitalize every letter that is capitalized in the originall?
- ☐ include every punctuation mark in the original?

Singular & Plural Verbs

*You have learned how to make nouns and pronouns singular or plural. Verbs also can be **singular** or **plural**. If a verb tells the action, state, or being of a singular noun, the verb is singular also. If it tells the action, state, or being a plural noun or pronoun, the verb is plural also. Just like nouns, many verbs must change form to show whether they are singular or plural.*

Rewrite each of these sentences, changing the underlined singular nouns or pronouns to plural, and changing the italicized verb as needed. Change any other words necessary so that the sentence makes complete sense.

The <u>carpenter</u> *found* a <u>piece</u> of wood.

_____

<u>Logs</u> *are put* on <u>fires</u>.

_____

A <u>piece</u> of wood *was found* in the <u>shop</u>.

_____

<u>I</u> *shall use* <u>it</u> to make the <u>leg</u> of a <u>table</u>.

_____

Week 4 • Day 2

Today is _____
                    Day   Date   Year

Nature Study

Read The Little Dipper and Polaris *(found in* Teaching Helps*)*

Sketch a picture of the **Big Dipper** *and the* **Little Dipper** *below. Label Polaris. Try to observe these in the night sky this week.*

Nature Notebook: Were you able to see the Big Dipper and the Little Dipper in the night sky this week? If so, draw them from your own observation. Place a compass rose in the correct orientation on your drawing. Also, remember to keep up your moon phases calendar.

Week 4 • Day 2

Copybook

Copy the fifth paragraph from this week's copybook selection into your copybook. Check your work, word by word, against the original.

Did you

☐ include every word in the original and spell every word correctly?
☐ capitalize every letter that is capitalized in the originall?
☐ include every punctuation mark in the original?

Suffixes: Two-Syllable Base Words

Rule to Review: When adding a suffix beginning with a vowel to a two-syllable word, double the final consonant if

✓ the word ends in one vowel then one consonant that you can see AND hear
✓ the accent is on the last syllable

Add the indicated suffix to these words.

happen + -ed	common + -ly	winter + -ize
permit + -ing	prefer + -ed	worship + -er
mumble + -ing	renew + -al	disobey + -ing

Choose two of the words you wrote above, and use them in original sentences.

Week 4 • Day 3

Today is _____
                    Day   Date   Year

Read And Narrate

The First Printer
~ *Thirty More Famous Stories Retold* by James Baldwin

Vocabulary to study before you read:

quaint	trudged	rarity
consequence	lodging	scarcely
dupes	degraded	plentiful
condition	rapid	coster
queer	acquaintance	

Draw a picture or series of pictures illustrating the story.

Week 4 • Day 3

Copybook

Copy the final two paragraphs and the attribution from this week's copybook selection into your copybook. Check your work, word by word, against the original.

Did you

❑ include every word in the original and spell every word correctly?

❑ capitalize every letter that is capitalized in the originall?

❑ include every punctuation mark in the original?

Verb Review

Rewrite the sentence twice, changing the underlined verb to the indicated tense.

The old carpenter was filled with joy.

Present _____

Future _____

Rewrite the sentence, changing the underlined singular noun or pronoun to plural, and changing the italicized verb as needed. Change any other words necessary so that the sentence makes complete sense.

He *rubs* his hands together happily.

_____

Homonyms, Synonyms, & Antonyms

Write:

a homonym for wood _____

a synonym for carpenter _____

an antonym for joy _____

Week 4 • Day 4

Today is _____
             Day   *Date*   *Year*

Picture Study _____

DICTATION

_____
_____
_____
_____
_____
_____
_____

SPELLING RULE: I BEFORE E

*Use **i** before **e**, except after **c**, and when it says /ā/ as in **neighbor**. There are some exceptions to this rule, but since **ie** is the most common usage when these two letters are paired, it is a helpful rule to know. Find the word in this week's copybook selection that follows the **i** before **e** rule, and use it in a sentence.*

_____

_____

*Here are a few exceptions to the the **i** before **e** rule. Copy these and memorize them.*

either	sovereign	forfeit
neither	height	foreign
protein	weird	leisure

Drawing Page

Stopping By Woods

Whose woods these are I think I know.
His house is in the village though;
He will not see me stopping here
To watch his woods fill up with snow.

My little horse must think it queer
To stop without a farmhouse near
Between the woods and frozen lake
The darkest evening of the year.

He gives his harness bells a shake
To ask if there is some mistake.
The only other sound's the sweep
Of easy wind and downy flake.

The woods are lovely, dark and deep.
But I have promises to keep,
And miles to go before I sleep,
And miles to go before I sleep.

~ Robert Frost

Week 5 • Day 1

Today is _____
      Day   *Date*   *Year*

James Watt and the Teakettle
~ *Thirty More Famous Stories Retold* by James Baldwin

Vocabulary to study before you read:

presently	preparations	heed
query	vapor	visible
profitable	inquisitive	yawning
harness	persevered	

Draw a picture or series of pictures illustrating the story.

COPYBOOK

Copy the title and first stanza from this week's copybook selection into your copybook. Check your work, word by word, against the original.

Did you

- ❑ include every word in the original and spell every word correctly?
- ❑ capitalize every letter that is capitalized in the originall?
- ❑ include every punctuation mark in the original?

SUBJECTS & PREDICATES

In the blanks on the left, write the noun or pronoun that tells who or what each of the following sentences is about.

house	His house <u><u>is</u></u> in the village.
_____	Snow fills the woods.
_____	My horse gives his harness bells a shake.
_____	The woods are lovely, dark and deep.
_____	I have promises to keep.

The **noun** or **pronoun** which you wrote in each blank above is the subject of the sentence. The **subject noun (or pronoun)** tells who or what the sentence is about.

The **predicate** tells what the subject is or does. Go back to the sentences above, and double underline the **verb** in the predicate that tells what the subject is or does.

Write one sentence with *village* as its subject and another with *snow* as its subject.

_____

_____

_____

Week 5 • Day 2

Today is _____
          Day   Date   Year

Nature Study

Read Cassiopeia (found in Teaching Helps).

*Sketch a picture of the **Big Dipper**, the **Little Dipper**, and **Cassiopeia** below. Label Polaris. Try to observe these in the night sky this week.*

Nature Notebook: Were you able to see Cassiopeia in the night sky this week? If so, draw it along with the Big Dipper and Little Dipper from your own observation. Label Polaris. Place a compass rose in the correct orientation on your drawing. Also, remember to keep up your moon phases calendar.

Week 5 • Day 2

Copybook

Copy the second and third stanzas from this week's copybook selection into your copybook. Check your work, word by word, against the original.

Did you

❑ include every word in the original and spell every word correctly?
❑ capitalize every letter that is capitalized in the originall?
❑ include every punctuation mark in the original?

Rhyming Words

The first three stanzas of this week's poem has a set of three rhyming words at the end of the first, second, and fourth lines. The word at the end of the second line does not rhyme with the words in its own stanza, but it rhymes with the set of three rhyming words from the next stanza. All of the words at the end of the fourth stanza rhyme. Why do you think the poet made the rhyme pattern of the final stanza different from the first three?

Write the three rhyming words from the first stanza.

Write the next four rhyming words—one from the first stanza, and three from the second.

Write the next four rhyming words—one from the second stanza, and three from the third.

Write the next four rhyming words—one from the third stanza, and three from the fourth. One is repeated; you do not need to write it twice.

47

Week 5 ♦ Day 3

Today is _____
          Day   Date   Year

Read And Narrate
_____

Dr. Johnson and His Father
~ *Thirty More Famous Stories Retold* by James Baldwin

Vocabulary to study before you read:

feeble	exertion	beseeching
wares	eaves	chaise
alights	seamed	asthma
ponderous	parish	lunatic
lull	venture	renowned

Draw a picture or series of pictures illustrating the story.

Copybook

Copy the last stanza and the attribution from this week's copybook selection into your copybook. Check your work, word by word, against the original.

Did you

- ❏ include every word in the original and spell every word correctly?
- ❏ capitalize every letter that is capitalized in the originall?
- ❏ include every punctuation mark in the original?

Subjects & Predicates

*Underline the **subject** of these sentences, then double underline the **predicate verb**. Rewrite the sentence twice, changing the predicate verb to the indicated tense.*

He will not see me here.

Present _____

Past _____

*Underline the **subject** of these sentences, then double underline the **predicate verb**. Rewrite each sentence, making the **subject** plural, and changing the **predicate** as needed. Change other words as needed so that the sentence makes complete sense.*

He stops without a farmhouse near.

_____

I have miles to go.

_____

Personification & Onomatopoeia

*In the second and third stanzas of this week's copybook selection, there are several examples of **personification**. Discuss this with your teacher. Also, look for the **onomatopoeia** (word whose sound gives a clue to its meaning - in this case, it is an imitation of a particular sound) in the third stanza.*

Week 5 ♦ Day 4

Today is _____
      Day   *Date*   *Year*

Picture Study

Week 5 ♦ Day 4

DICTATION

_____
_____
_____
_____
_____
_____

CONTRACTIONS

A contraction shortens a group of words by replacing a letter or letters with an apostrophe (').

   do not = don't

Write the contraction for each group of words. The last one is a bit tricky.

I have	_____
cannot	_____
must not	_____
it is	_____
will not	_____

Write the contraction found in this week's poem. Then, write the two words that are shortened to form this contraction.

Drawing Page

A Laconic Answer

Many miles beyond Rome there was a famous country which we call Greece. The people of Greece were not united like the Romans; but instead there were several states, each of which had its own rulers. Some of the people in the southern part of the country were called Spartans, and they were noted for their simple habits and their bravery. The name of their land was Laconia, and so they were sometimes called Lacons.

One of the strange rules which the Spartans had, was that they should speak briefly, and never use more words than were needed. And so a short answer is often spoken of as being *laconic*; that is, as being such an answer as a Lacon would be likely to give.

There was in the northern part of Greece a land called Macedon; and this land was at one time ruled over by a war-like king named Philip. Philip of Macedon wanted to become the master of all Greece. So he raised a great army, and made war upon the other states, until nearly all of them were forced to call him their king. Then he sent a letter to the Spartans in Laconia, and said, "If I go down into your country, I will level your great city to the ground."

In a few days, an answer was brought back to him. When he opened the letter, he found only one word written there.

That word was "IF."

It was as much as to say, "We are not afraid of you so long as the little word 'if' stands in your way."

~ James Baldwin

Week 6 • Day 1

Today is _____
　　　　　　　　Day　　　　　　　　　Date　　　　　　　　Year

Webster and the Woodchuck
~ *Thirty More Famous Stories Retold* by James Baldwin

Vocabulary to study before you read:

lawyer	burrow	tender
cunning	mischief	pitied
settle	plead	prosecutor
tremble	stirred	

Draw a picture or series of pictures illustrating the story.

Week 6 • Day 1

Copybook

Copy the title and the second paragraph* from this week's copybook selection into your copybook. Check your work, word by word, against the original.

Did you

- ❑ include every word in the original and spell every word correctly?
- ❑ capitalize every letter that is capitalized in the originall?
- ❑ include every punctuation mark in the original?

Correct Use of Words: Shall & Will

Thus far, we have used the verb will *to indicate simple future tense. When the subject of a sentence is either* I *or* we, *the verb* shall *should generally be used instead. The verb* will *is often used with* I *or* we; *however, it is properly used only when we wish to show strong determination.*

    We shall learn more about Sparta.

    We will be brave.

Underline the **subject** *of these sentences, then double underline the* **predicate verb**. *Rewrite each sentence twice to indicate simple future tense. Use* shall *in the first sentence of each set and* will *in the second. Discuss the different meaning of each with your teacher.*

    I level your great city to the ground.

_____

_____

    We do not fear Philip of Macedon. (Note: not *is NOT part of the verb.*)

_____

_____

**Due to the length of this selection, the first paragraph is not included in the copybook for this week.*

Week 6 • Day 2

Today is _____
            Day   Date   Year

Nature Study

Read Orion and the Pleiades (found in Teaching Helps). Also read Job 9:9, Job 38:31, and Amos 5:8.

Sketch a picture of the Orion and Taurus below. Label the Pleiades. Try to observe them in the night sky this week.

Nature Notebook: Were you able to see Orion and Taurus in the night sky this week? If so, draw them from your own observation. Label the Pleiades. Place a compass rose in the correct orientation on your drawing. Also, remember to keep up your moon phases calendar.

Copybook

Copy the third paragraph from this week's copybook selection into your copybook. Check your work, word by word, against the original.

Did you

❑ include every word in the original and spell every word correctly?

❑ capitalize every letter that is capitalized in the originall?

❑ include every punctuation mark in the original?

Suffixes: Base Word Ending in Silent E

*Rule to Review: Words that end with a silent **e** drop the **e** when adding a suffix that begins with a vowel, unless dropping the **e** interferes with some other rule.*

Add the indicated suffix to these words. Write is tricky — say it aloud with the suffix.

mile + -age	unite + -ing	rule + -er
brave + -ry	strange + -ly	give + -en
raise + -ing	state + -ing	state + -ment
write + -er	acre + -age	force + -able

Choose two of the words you wrote above, and use them in original sentences.

Week 6 • Day 3

Today is _____
　　　　　　　Day　　　　　　　　　Date　　　　　　　　Year

Read And Narrate
_____

"As Rich As Croesus"
~ *Thirty More Famous Stories Retold* by James Baldwin

Vocabulary to study before you read:

famed	contented	noted
orchards	labored	manfully
toiled	nobly	misfortunes
overthrowing	petty	handling
timber	pyre	soothe

Draw a picture or series of pictures illustrating the story.

Week 6 • Day 3

Copybook

Copy the fourth through sixth paragraphs and the attribution from this week's copybook selection into your copybook. Check your work, word by word, against the original.

Did you

❏ include every word in the original and spell every word correctly?
❏ capitalize every letter that is capitalized in the originall?
❏ include every punctuation mark in the original?

Subjects & Predicates

*Underline the **subject** of this sentence, then double underline the **predicate verb**. Rewrite the sentence twice, changing the verb to the indicated tense.*

Philip raises a great army.

Past _____

Future _____

*Underline the **subject** of this sentence, then double underline the **predicate verb**. Rewrite the sentence with a plural **subject**. Change the **predicate verb** as needed. Change any other words necessary so that the sentence makes complete sense.*

A laconic answer is a brief answer.

Writing a Friendly letter

Write a thank you letter to someone who has done you a kindness. Some suggestions: your pastor, librarian, sports coach, or anyone else who has helped or served you in some way. If you need a refresher on writing a letter, see The Parts of A Friendly Letter *and* The Envelope *in the Appendix.*

Write the name of the person to whom you wrote.

Week 6 ◆ Day 4

Today is _____
　　　　　　　　　Day　　　　　　　Date　　　　　　　Year

Picture Study _____

Dictation

_____
_____
_____
_____
_____
_____

Derivatives

What is the name of the land where the Spartans lived? _____

What is the other name by which Spartans were known? _____

What is a brief answer called? _____

Homonyms, Synonyms, & Antonyms

Write:

   a homonym for Greece _____

   a homonym for raise _____

   a synonym for brief _____

   an antonym for brief _____

   a synonym for master _____

Drawing Page

Our God, Our Help In Ages Past

Our God, our help in ages past,
Our hope for years to come,
Our shelter from the stormy blast,
And our eternal home.

Under the shadow of Thy throne
Thy saints have dwelt secure;
Sufficient is Thine arm alone,
And our defense is sure.

Before the hills in order stood,
Or earth received her frame,
From everlasting Thou art God,
To endless years the same.

A thousand ages in Thy sight
Are like an evening gone;
Short as the watch that ends the night
Before the rising sun.

Time, like an ever-rolling stream,
Bears all its sons away;
They fly forgotten, as a dream
Dies at the opening day.

Our God, our help in ages past,
Our hope for years to come,
Be Thou our guard while troubles last,
And our eternal home.

~ Isaac Watts

Week 7 • Day 1

Today is _____
                    Day   Date   Year

The Gordian Knot
~ *Thirty More Famous Stories Retold* by James Baldwin

Vocabulary to study before you read:

region	quarries	vineyards
grieved	affairs	oracle
bewildered	uproar	slew
deftly	oppose	

Draw a picture or series of pictures illustrating the story.

Week 7 ♦ Day 1

Copybook

Copy the title and first two stanzas from this week's copybook selection into your copybook. Check your work, word by word, against the original.

Did you

❏ include every word in the original and spell every word correctly?
❏ capitalize every letter that is capitalized in the originall?
❏ include every punctuation mark in the original?

Verb Tense: Past, Present, & Future

In addition to the tense of the verb, other words in the sentence can indicate the time of the action, being, or state.

Add a subject and predicate verb from this week's copybook selection to these opening words to make a complete sentence. Make sure the predicate verb is in the appropriate tense.

In ages past, _____

For years to come, _____

On this day, _____

Ever afterwards, _____

For each of these sentences, write appropriate opening words. Make sure the predicate verb is in the appropriate tense. Put a comma after the opening word(s).*

_____ there was a country called Greece.

_____ the woods are filling up with snow.

_____ I shall make the leg of a table!

_____ Tarva salutes Alambil.

* *See Primer Two Teaching Helps for time expression ideas.*

Week 7 • Day 2

Today is _____
       Day   Date   Year

Nature Study

Review the characteristics of birds:

- ✓ have a backbone (vertebrates)
- ✓ are warm-blooded
- ✓ have lungs that breathe air
- ✓ are covered with feathers
- ✓ have wings
- ✓ lay eggs

List 10 kinds of birds:

1. _____
2. _____
3. _____
4. _____
5. _____
6. _____
7. _____
8. _____
9. _____
10. _____

Week 7 • Day 2

Copybook

Copy the third and fourth stanzas from this week's copybook selection into your copybook. Check your work, word by word, against the original.

Did you

- ❏ include every word in the original and spell every word correctly?
- ❏ capitalize every letter that is capitalized in the originall?
- ❏ include every punctuation mark in the original?

Rhyming Words

Each stanza of this hymn has a pair of rhyming words at the end of the first and third lines, and another pair in the second and fourth lines.

Write the rhyming sets or pairs from this week's poem with endings that are spelled the same.

_____

_____

_____

_____

Write the rhyming words from the poem with endings that are spelled differently.

_____

_____

*Write several words that rhyme with **bears**. Try to write at least three with an ending that is spelled differently.*

_____

Week 7 • Day 3

Today is _____
　　　　　Day　　　　　　　　Date　　　　　　　Year

Read And Narrate

Why Alexander Wept
~ *Thirty More Famous Stories Retold* by James Baldwin

Vocabulary to study before you read:

- overran
- desolate
- trackless
- bounds
- marshes
- inhabited
- plains
- tangled

Draw a picture or series of pictures illustrating the story.

Copybook

Copy the final two stanzas and the attribution from this week's copybook selection into your copybook. Check your work, word by word, against the original.

Did you

- ❏ include every word in the original and spell every word correctly?
- ❏ capitalize every letter that is capitalized in the originall?
- ❏ include every punctuation mark in the original?

Subjects & Predicates

*Underline the **subject** of this sentence, then double underline the **predicate verb**. Rewrite the sentence twice, changing the verb to the indicated tense.*

God is our shelter and our eternal home.

Past _____

Future _____

*Underline the **subject** of this sentence, then double underline the **predicate verb**. Rewrite the sentence making the **subject** plural, and changing the **predicate verb** as needed. Change any other words necessary so that the sentence makes complete sense.*

The night watch is short.

_____

Writing a Friendly Letter

Write to a family member or friend who lives far away. Tell what you have been learning about birds in Nature Study. If needed, refer to The Parts of A Friendly Letter and The Envelope in the Appendix.

Write the name of the person to whom you wrote.

_____

Week 7 • Day 4

Today is _____
                        Day   *Date*   *Year*

Picture Study _____

Dictation

___

Onomatopoeia & Simile

*Find the **onomatopoeia** in the first stanza, and write it on the line.*

___

*Find a **simile** in this week's copybook selection. Remember that a simile compares two things that are not usually associated with one another using the words like, as, or than. Write the two things being compared.*

_____ is compared to _____

*Look and listen for **similes** in your reading this week, and write a few here.*

___

Drawing Page

from The Children's Book of Birds

Each bird mother has her own way of making the nest, but there is one thing almost all of them try to do, and that is to hide it.

They cannot put their little homes out in plain sight, as we do our houses, because so many creatures want to rob them. Squirrels and snakes and rats, and some big birds, and cats and many others, like to eat eggs and young birds.

So most birds try, first of all, to find good hiding-places. Some tiny warblers go to the tops of the tallest trees, and hide the nest among the leaves. Orioles hang the swinging cradle at the end of a branch, where cats and snakes and naughty boys cannot come. Song sparrows tuck the little home in a tuft of weeds, on the ground, and bobolinks hide it in the deep grass.

After a safe place is found, they have to get something to build of. They hunt all about and gather small twigs, or grass stems, or fine rootlets, and pull narrow strips of bark off the grapevines and the birch-trees, or they pick up strings and horsehairs, and many other things. Robins and swallows use mud.

~ Olive Thorne Miller

Week 8 • Day 1

Today is _____
                Day   Date   Year

Frederick Barbarossa
~ Thirty More Famous Stories Retold by James Baldwin

Vocabulary to study before you read:

score	subdued	imperial
ambition	devout	crusade
torrent	precipice	mail
lamenting	beckoned	immortals
toll	boughs	linden
inlaid	ranged	entranced

Draw a picture or series of pictures illustrating the story.

COPYBOOK

Copy the title and first two paragraphs from this week's copybook selection into your copybook. Check your work, word by word, against the original.

Did you

❑ include every word in the original and spell every word correctly?

❑ capitalize every letter that is capitalized in the originall?

❑ include every punctuation mark in the original?

CONJUNCTIONS

Write the word and in the blanks of the first sentence, the word but in the blank of the second sentence, and the word or in the blanks of the third sentence.

Squirrels _____ snakes _____ rats like to eat eggs _____ young birds

Each kind of bird builds its own kind of nest, _____ all birds hide their nests.

The nest is built of twigs from trees _____ stems of grass _____ pieces of string.

And, but, and or are **conjunctions** *in these sentences.* **Conjunctions** *join words or groups of words.*

Circle the conjunctions and, but, and or in these sentences. Tell your teacher whether they join words or groups of words.

Birds cannot put their little homes out in plain sight, but they must hide them.

They hide their nests in treetops, or at the end of a branch, or in a tuft of weeds, or in the deep grass.

Robins and swallows build their nests with mud.

Write a sentence using the verbs build *and* hide, *and the conjunction* and.

_____

_____

Week 8 • Day 2

Today is _____
                   Day   Date   Year

Nature Study

Choose a bird and talk about its characteristics, covering these points. Then sketch the bird in the frame. Sketch a close-up of its beak also.

- ❏ Its size
- ❏ Its body covering
- ❏ Its food
- ❏ Its means of protecting itself
- ❏ Its habits

Write the bird's English and Latin names:

_____

_____

Nature Noteboook: Draw and color a more detailed picture of the bird and its beak. Include its English and Latin names.

76

Copybook

Copy the third paragraph from this week's copybook selection into your copybook. Check your work, word by word, against the original.

Did you

❑ include every word in the original and spell every word correctly?
❑ capitalize every letter that is capitalized in the originall?
❑ include every punctuation mark in the original?

Noun Review

From this week's copybook selection:

Write three common nouns that name birds, and three that name mammals.

_____

_____

Write three common nouns that name places.

_____

The Business Letter

Because handwritten business letters are quickly becoming a rarity in our electronic age, you may be more likely to get a personal reply if you take the time to write one. Study the standard format of the business letter in the Appendix.

Write a business letter to an orgainization requesting information about a subject you are studying. For example, you might write to the National Zoo to obtain more information about birds.

Write the name of the organization to whom you wrote and the request you made.

_____

Week 8 • Day 3

Today is _____
                   Day   Date   Year

Read And Narrate

King John and Magna Charta
~ Thirty More Famous Stories Retold by James Baldwin

Vocabulary to study before you read:

dominions	barons	offended
grievances	submit	archbishop
privileges	charter	gestures
wage	oath	raved
thither	boroughs	gnawed

Draw a picture or series of pictures illustrating the story.

Week 8 • Day 3

Copybook

Copy the fourth paragraph and the attribution from this week's copybook selection into your copybook. Check your work, word by word, against the original.

Did you

❑ include every word in the original and spell every word correctly?

❑ capitalize every letter that is capitalized in the originall?

❑ include every punctuation mark in the original?

Subjects & Predicates

*Underline the **subject** of this sentence, then double underline the **predicate verb**. Rewrite the sentence twice, changing the verb to the indicated tense.*

The warbler builds her nest in a tree.

Past _____

Future _____

*Underline the **subject** of these sentences, then double underline the **predicate verb**. Rewrite the sentences, changing the **subject** to singular, and changing the **predicate** as needed. Change any other words necessary so that the sentence makes complete sense.*

Mother birds hide their nests.

_____

Sparrows tuck their nests in a tuft of weeds.

_____

Safe places are found.

_____

Week 8 ♦ Day 4

Today is _____
    Day   Date   Year

Picture Study _____

Dictation

Homonyms, Synonyms, & Antonyms

Write:

a homonym for sight _____

a homonym for plain _____

a synonym for rob _____

an antonym for naughty _____

a synonym for many _____

an antonym for narrow _____

Write an original sentence using one synonym, one antomym, and one homonym you wrote above.

Drawing Page

from The Wind

I saw you toss the kites on high

And blow the birds about the sky;

And all around I heard you pass,

Like ladies' skirts across the grass--

    O wind, a-blowing all day long,

    O wind, that sings so loud a song!

I saw the different things you did,

But always you yourself you hid.

I felt you push, I heard you call,

I could not see yourself at all--

    O wind, a-blowing all day long,

    O wind, that sings so loud a song!

O you that are so strong and cold,

O blower, are you young or old?

Are you a beast of field and tree,

Or just a stronger child than me?

    O wind, a-blowing all day long,

    O wind, that sings so loud a song!

~ Robert Louis Stevenson

Week 9 • Day 1

Today is _____
               Day   Date   Year

The Fall of Troy (Chapters I and II)
~ *Thirty More Famous Stories Retold* by James Baldwin

Vocabulary to study before you read:

hosts	conquest	vengeance
breastwork	prevail	shrewdest
discern	forges	implements
overhauled	soothsayers	crockery
thong	valiantly	maimed
fain	atone	eluded

Draw a picture or series of pictures illustrating the story.

Week 9 • Day 1

Copybook

Copy the title and first stanza from this week's copybook selection into your copybook. Check your work, word by word, against the original.

Did you

❑ include every word in the original and spell every word correctly?

❑ capitalize every letter that is capitalized in the originall?

❑ include every punctuation mark in the original?

Pronouns & Personification

Remember, there are two ways that an author can create personification:

✓ Inanimate objects are given qualities or actions of living things

✓ Non-humans are given human characteristics or actions

In The Wind, *the poet personifies the wind by speaking directly to it—giving it the human quality of being able to hear and understand.*

I saw YOU toss the kite on high...

Another poet has personified the wind, using the pronoun I, giving the wind a human voice and human thoughts to tell about itself in the poem:

I whirl the leaves in flocks of brown, And send them high and low.

Rewrite these lines as if the wind were speaking to you with a human voice and human thoughts. (Hint: use the pronoun I.)

You toss the kite on high. You blow the birds about the sky.

_____

_____

Find the simile in the first stanza (look for like, as, *or* than). *What is compared?*

_____ is compared to _____

Week 9 • Day 2

Today is _____
       Day   Date   Year

Nature Study

Choose a bird and talk about its characteristics, covering these points. Then sketch the bird in the frame. Sketch a close-up of its beak also.

- ❑ Its size
- ❑ Its body covering
- ❑ Its food
- ❑ Its means of protecting itself
- ❑ Its habits

Write the bird's English and Latin names:

_____

_____

Nature Noteboook: Draw and color a more detailed picture of the bird and its beak. Include its English and Latin names.

Week 9 ♦ Day 2

Copybook

Copy the second stanza from this week's copybook selection into your copybook. Check your work, word by word, against the original.

Did you

❑ include every word in the original and spell every word correctly?

❑ capitalize every letter that is capitalized in the originall?

❑ include every punctuation mark in the original?

Rhyming Words

Each stanza of this hymn has a pair of rhyming words at the end of the first and second lines, another pair in the third and fourth lines, and one more pair in the fifth and sixth lines.

Write the rhyming words from this week's poem with endings that are spelled the same.

_____

_____

_____

_____

Write the rhyming words from the poem with endings that are spelled differently.

_____

_____

*Write several words that rhyme with **blowing**. Try to write at least two with an ending that is spelled differently.*

_____

_____

Week 9 • Day 3

Today is _____
             Day   Date   Year

Read And Narrate

The Fall of Troy (Chapters III and IV)
~ *Thirty More Famous Stories Retold* by James Baldwin

Vocabulary to study before you read:

rabble	undermine	rearing
emerged	forthwith	intent
stealthily	coping	panel
encased	moored	wiles
siege		

Draw a picture or series of pictures illustrating the story.

Copybook

Copy the final stanza and the attribution from this week's copybook selection into your copybook. Check your work, word by word, against the original.

Did you

- ❏ include every word in the original and spell every word correctly?
- ❏ capitalize every letter that is capitalized in the originall?
- ❏ include every punctuation mark in the original?

Subjects & Predicates

*Underline the **subject** of this sentence, then double underline the **predicate verb**. Rewrite the sentence twice, changing the verb to the indicated tense.*

You sing so loud a song!

Past _____

Future _____

*Underline the **subject** of this sentence, then double underline the **predicate verb**. Rewrite the sentence, changing the **subject** to singular, and changing the **predicate** as needed. Change any other words necessary so that the sentence makes complete sense. Pay particular attention to the possessive pronoun which will need to be changed.*

Ladies' skirts rustle across the grass.

_____

The Business Letter

Write a letter of commendation to a business which has provided excellent service. For example, if you received excellent service from a server at a restaurant, write a letter telling the owner of the business about it.

Write the name of the business to whom you wrote.

_____

Week 9 • Day 4

Today is _____
                       Day   Date   Year

Picture Study

Dictation

Nouns & Pronoun Review

Rewrite this sentence. For the underlined noun, substitute an appropriate pronoun. For the underlined pronoun, substitute the appropriate noun.

<u>He</u> felt <u>the wind</u> push and call.

Write the alternate possessive form.

skirts of ladies

kites' tails

push of the wind

poems' titles

homes of sparrows

boys' mischief

Drawing Page

from Heidi

"Why do the mountains have no names, grandfather?" asked Heidi.

"They all have names, and if you tell me their shape I can name them for you."

Heidi described several and the old man could name them all. The child told him now about all the happenings of the day, and especially about the wonderful fire. She asked how it came about.

"The sun does it," he exclaimed. "Saying good-night to the mountains, he throws his most beautiful rays to them, that they may not forget him till the morning."

Heidi was so much pleased with this explanation, that she could hardly wait to see the sun's good-night greetings repeated. It was time now to go to bed, and Heidi slept soundly all night. She dreamt that the little Snowhopper was bounding happily about on the glowing mountains with many glistening roses blooming round her.

~ Johanna Spyri

Week 10 • Day 1

Today is _____
　　　　　　　Day　　　　　　　　　　Date　　　　　　　　　Year

How Rome Was Founded (Chapters I-IV)
~ *Thirty More Famous Stories Retold* by James Baldwin

Vocabulary to study before you read:

pike	barbarous	mutton
seldom	priestess	lowlands
eddying	trough	brushwood
underwood	whelps	driftwood
lapped		

Draw a picture or series of pictures illustrating the story.

Week 10 • Day 1

Copybook

Copy the title and first two paragraphs from this week's copybook selection into your copybook. Check your work, word by word, against the original.

Did you

☐ include every word in the original and spell every word correctly?
☐ capitalize every letter that is capitalized in the originall?
☐ include every punctuation mark in the original?

Questions & Word Order

In very many sentences, the **subject** *comes before the* **predicate verb**. *But sometimes, the* **predicate verb** *will come first. This is often the case with sentences which ask questions. Find and underline the subjects of these sentences by asking who or what the sentence is about. Then find and double underline the predicate verb by asking what the subject is or does.*

Do the mountains have names?

Are you a beast of field or tree?

Rewrite each question as a statement with the subject at the beginning.

_____

_____

Underline the subject and double underline the predicate verb in these statements.

He could name them for her.

Snowhopper was bounding happily about.

Rewrite each statement as a question with a verb at the beginning.

_____

_____

Week 10 • Day 2

Today is _____
        Day   Date   Year

Nature Study

Choose a bird and talk about its characteristics, covering these points. Then sketch the bird in the frame. Sketch a close-up of its beak also.

- ❑ Its size
- ❑ Its body covering
- ❑ Its food
- ❑ Its means of protecting itself
- ❑ Its habits

Write the bird's English and Latin names:

_____

_____

Nature Noteboook: Draw and color a more detailed picture of the bird and its beak. Include its English and Latin names.

Week 10 • Day 2

Copybook

Copy the third and fourth paragraphs from this week's copybook selection into your copybook. Check your work, word by word, against the original.

Did you

❑ include every word in the original and spell every word correctly?
❑ capitalize every letter that is capitalized in the originall?
❑ include every punctuation mark in the original?

Suffixes: Changing y to i

*Rule to Review: Words that end with a single vowel **y** often exchange the **y** for an **i** before adding a suffix, unless the suffix begins with **-i**. To make them plural, add **-es**.*

Example: **puppy,** change **y → i + -es = puppies**

Add the suffix or change the word form as indicated.

happy + -ness	say + -ing	sky *(make plural)*
fancy + -er	duty + -ful	leaf *(make plural)*
fire *(make past)*	sound + -ly	time + -ing
valley *(make plural)*	birch *(make plural)*	happen + -ing

Choose two of the words you wrote above, and use them in an original sentence.

Week 10 • Day 3

Today is _____
         Day   Date   Year

Read And Narrate

How Rome Was Founded (Chapters V-VIII)
~ *Thirty More Famous Stories Retold* by James Baldwin

Vocabulary to study before you read:

withering	bethought	foster
valor	enterprise	excursion
tethered	ado	trespassed
soiled	leave	augurs
hinder	sneered	

Draw a picture or series of pictures illustrating the story.

Week 10 • Day 3

Copybook

Copy the final paragraph and the attribution from this week's copybook selection into your copybook. Check your work, word by word, against the original.

Did you

❑ include every word in the original and spell every word correctly?
❑ capitalize every letter that is capitalized in the originall?
❑ include every punctuation mark in the original?

Subjects & Predicates

*Underline the **subject** of this sentence, then double underline the **predicate verb**. Rewrite the sentence twice, changing the verb to the indicated tense. Change the time expression* (this night) *to match the verb tense.*

Heidi sleeps soundly this night.

Past _____

Future _____

*Underline the **subject** of this sentence, then double underline the **predicate verb**. Rewrite the sentence, changing the **subject** to singular, and changing the **predicate verb** as needed. Change other words as needed so that the sentence makes complete sense. Note that the possessive noun is not the subject.*

Are the sun's greetings repeated?

_____

The Business Letter

Write a letter to an elected official or public servant. You might write to thank him or her for serving, or you might write about an issue that is important to you.

Write the name of the official to whom you wrote.

_____

Week 10 • Day 4

Today is _____
                     Day   *Date*   *Year*

Picture Study

Week 10 • Day 4

Dictation

_____

_____

_____

_____

_____

_____

_____

Homonyms, Synonyms, & Antonyms

Write:

a *homonym* for night   _____

a *homonym* for wait   _____

a *synonym* for wonderful   _____

an *antonym* for beautiful   _____

a *synonym* for asked   _____

an *antonym* for blooming   _____

Write an original sentence using the synonyms you wrote above.

_____

_____

Drawing Page

All Glory, Laud, and Honor

All glory, laud, and honor,
To Thee, Redeemer, King,
To whom the lips of children
Made sweet hosannas ring!
Thou art the King of Israel,
Thou David's royal Son,
Who in the Lord's name comest,
The King and Blessèd One.

The people of the Hebrews
With palms before Thee went;
Our praise and prayer and anthems
Before Thee we present:
To Thee, before Thy passion,
They sang their hymns of praise;
To Thee, now high exalted,
Our melody we raise.

Thou didst accept their praises;
Accept the prayers we bring,
Who in all good delightest,
Thou good and gracious King!
All glory, laud, and honor
To Thee, Redeemer, King,
To whom the lips of children
Made sweet hosannas ring!

~ Theodulph of Orleans (translated by John Mason Neale)

Week 11 • Day 1

Today is _____
                    Day   Date   Year

How Decius Mus Saved Rome
~ Thirty More Famous Stories Retold by James Baldwin

Vocabulary to study before you read:

encamped	maiden	destiny
heed	utterly	waver
fray	contesting	dignity
javelin	thrust	grappling

Draw a picture or series of pictures illustrating the story.

Week 11 • Day 1

Copybook

Copy the title and first stanza from this week's copybook selection into your copybook. Check your work, word by word, against the original.

Did you

    ❑ include every word in the original and spell every word correctly?
    ❑ capitalize every letter that is capitalized in the originall?
    ❑ include every punctuation mark in the original?

Conjunctions & Commas

This sentence has three subjects, but only one predicate verb. Underline the subjects, and double underline the verb.

    All glory and laud and honor are given to the Lord.

As you can see in this week's copybook selection, words in a series like this are often written with commas between each word of the series. The conjunction appears only before the final word in the series. Notice there is also a comma before that conjunction.

Rewrite this sentence from the copybook selection as a series separated by commas, and with only one conjunction:

    Our praise and prayers and anthems we present.

_____

Write a sentence telling three names (single-word) used for Jesus in this hymn. Use commas and only one conjunction. Then, rewrite the sentence using conjunctions and no commas.

_____

_____

_____

_____

Week 11 • Day 2

Today is _____
                    Day   Date   Year

Nature Study

Choose a bird and talk about its characteristics, covering these points. Then sketch the bird in the frame. Sketch a close-up of its beak also.

- ❑ Its size
- ❑ Its body covering
- ❑ Its food
- ❑ Its means of protecting itself
- ❑ Its habits

Write the bird's English and Latin names:

_____

_____

Nature Noteboook: Draw and color a more detailed picture of the bird and its beak. Include its English and Latin names.

Week 11 • Day 2

Copybook

Copy the second stanza from this week's copybook selection into your copybook. Check your work, word by word, against the original.

Did you

- ❏ include every word in the original and spell every word correctly?
- ❏ capitalize every letter that is capitalized in the originall?
- ❏ include every punctuation mark in the original?

Rhyming Words

Find the rhyming words in this week's hymn.

Write the rhyming words with endings that are spelled the same.

_____

_____

_____

Write the rhyming words with endings that are spelled differently.

_____

*Write several words that rhyme with **sweet** and several that rhyme with **hymns**. Try to write at least two for each with an ending that is spelled differently.*

_____

_____

_____

Week 11 • Day 3

Today is _____
  Day   Date   Year

READ AND NARRATE

Delenda Est Carthago
~ *Thirty More Famous Stories Retold* by James Baldwin

Vocabulary to study before you read:

censor	ambassador	harbor
wharfs	merchandise	thronged
surpassed	estimated	toga
signified	self-indulgence	reproving
folly	prospects	fare

Draw a picture or series of pictures illustrating the story.

Week 11 • Day 3

Copybook

Copy the third stanza and the attribution from this week's copybook selection into your copybook. Check your work, word by word, against the original.

Did you

☐ include every word in the original and spell every word correctly?

☐ capitalize every letter that is capitalized in the originall?

☐ include every punctuation mark in the original?

Subjects & Predicates

*Underline the **subject** of this sentence, then double underline the **predicate verb**. Rewrite the sentence twice, changing the verb to the indicated tense. Add an appropriate time expression to match the verb tense. You may use the archaic pronoun and verb, or you may use the forms we would use today.*

Didst Thou accept their praises?

Present _____

Future _____

*Underline the **subject** of this sentence, then double underline the **predicate verb**. Rewrite the sentence, making the **subject** singular, and changing the **predicate** as needed. Change other words as needed so that the sentence makes complete sense.*

The children were singing sweet hosannas.

_____

Noun Review

From this week's copybook selection:

Write three proper nouns that name persons. Include modifiers that are part of a title.

Week 11 • Day 4

Today is _____
　　　　　　　Day　　　　　　　　*Date*　　　　　　　　*Year*

Picture Study

Week 11 • Day 4

Dictation

Homonyms, Synonyms, & Antonyms

Write:

a *homonym for* hymn

a *homonym for* all

a *synonym for* laud (noun)

an *antonym for* accept

a *synonym for* anthem

an *antonym for* gracious

Write an original sentence using the synonyms you wrote above.

Drawing Page

The Good Samaritan

But he, wanting to justify himself, said to Jesus, "And who is my neighbor?"

Then Jesus answered and said: "A certain man went down from Jerusalem to Jericho, and fell among thieves, who stripped him of his clothing, wounded him, and departed, leaving him half dead. Now by chance a certain priest came down that road. And when he saw him, he passed by on the other side. Likewise a Levite, when he arrived at the place, came and looked, and passed by on the other side. But a certain Samaritan, as he journeyed, came where he was. And when he saw him, he had compassion. So he went to him and bandaged his wounds, pouring on oil and wine; and he set him on his own animal, brought him to an inn, and took care of him. On the next day, when he departed, he took out two denarii, gave them to the innkeeper, and said to him, 'Take care of him; and whatever more you spend, when I come again, I will repay you.' So which of these three do you think was neighbor to him who fell among the thieves?"

And he said, "He who showed mercy on him."

Then Jesus said to him, "Go and do likewise."

~ Luke 10:29-37, New King James Version

Week 12 • Day 1

Today is _____
       Day   Date   Year

Hannibal, Hero of Carthage
~ *Thirty More Famous Stories Retold* by James Baldwin

Vocabulary to study before you read:

warehouses	principal	quays
embark	implore	procession
discordant	incense	daunted
cherish	rugged	chasm
vainly		

Draw a picture or series of pictures illustrating the story.

WEEK 12 • DAY 1

COPYBOOK

Copy the title and first paragraph from this week's copybook selection into your copybook. Check your work, word by word, against the original.

Did you

❏ include every word in the original and spell every word correctly?
❏ capitalize every letter that is capitalized in the originall?
❏ include every punctuation mark in the original?

SUBJECTS & PREDICATES

*Underline the **subject** of these sentences, then double underline the **predicate verb**. Rewrite each sentence twice, changing the verb to the indicated tense.*

Which man is neighbor?

Past _____

Future _____

A Levite came and looked.

Present _____

Future _____

*Underline the **subject** of each sentence, then double underline the **predicate verb**. Rewrite each sentence, making the **subject** singular, and changing the **predicate** as needed. Change other words as needed so that the sentence makes complete sense.*

Did theives strip him of his clothing?

_____

Parables teach truth.

Week 12 • Day 2

Today is _____
                      Day   Date   Year

NATURE STUDY

Choose a bird and talk about its characteristics, covering these points. Then sketch the bird in the frame. Sketch a close-up of its beak also.

- ❏ Its size
- ❏ Its body covering
- ❏ Its food
- ❏ Its means of protecting itself
- ❏ Its habits

Write the bird's English and Latin names:

_____

_____

Nature Noteboook: Draw and color a more detailed picture of the bird and its beak. Include its English and Latin names.

Week 12 ♦ Day 2

Copybook

Copy the second paragraph from this week's copybook selection into your copybook. Check your work, word by word, against the original.

Did you

☐ include every word in the original and spell every word correctly?

☐ capitalize every letter that is capitalized in the originall?

☐ include every punctuation mark in the original?

Conjunctions & Commas

Rewrite this sentence with a series separated by commas and with only one conjunction:

The thieves stripped him and wounded him and departed.

_____

Rewrite this sentence with a series joined with conjunctions and no commas:

Is the priest, the Levite, or the Samaritan the neighbor?

_____

Write a sentence with these words in a series. Use commas and only one conjunction. Then rewrite the sentence using conjunctions and no commas.

bandaged his wounds, brought him to an inn, took care of him

_____

_____

_____

Week 12 • Day 3

Today is _____
           Day   Date   Year

Read And Narrate

Crossing the Rubicon
~ Thirty More Famous Stories Retold by James Baldwin

Vocabulary to study before you read:

loyally	civilized	republic
induced	accusations	treason
legion	veterans	perils
enthusiastic	fatigue	strife
foresee	senators	litters

Draw a picture or series of pictures illustrating the story.

Week 12 • Day 3

Copybook

Copy the third paragraph and the attribution from this week's copybook selection into your copybook. Check your work, word by word, against the original.

Did you

☐ include every word in the original and spell every word correctly?
☐ capitalize every letter that is capitalized in the originall?
☐ include every punctuation mark in the original?

Suffixes: Review

Add the suffix or change the word form as indicated.

want *(make past)*	neighbor + -ly	cloth *(make plural)*
bandage + -ing	thief *(make plural)*	arrive + -ing
care + -less + -ness	mercy *(make plural)*	see *(make past)*
care + full + -ness	mercy + full + ly	journey *(make past)*

Choose four of the words you wrote above, and use them in one or two original sentences.

_____

_____

_____

_____

Week 12 • Day 4

Today is _____
             Day   Date   Year

Picture Study

Week 12 • Day 4

DICTATION

HOMONYMS, SYNONYMS, & ANTONYMS

Write:

a homonym for by _____

a homonym for wine _____

a synonym for wounded _____

an antonym for depart _____

a synonym for inn _____

an antonym for mercy _____

Write an original sentence using two or more of the words you wrote above.

Drawing Page

APPENDIX

The Parts of A Friendly Letter

Heading → 285 Cottage Way
Raven Hill, Virginia 12345
February 10, 2014

Dear Grandma,   ← Greeting (Salutation)

    We finally have some snow! I measured six inches out by the birdfeeder. The snow fell all night. I love the way it looks when it is snowing at night. It is so soft and pretty. Sometimes, when I look out the window it looks like the house is rising instead of the snow falling.
    Today when I woke up, it looked like a fairyland with the sun sparkling on the snow. ← Body
I could not wait to get outside. I made snow angels and a funny-looking snowman, and then we all had a huge snowball fight. After that, we came in and had hot chocolate and read by the fire with Mom.
    I miss you and Grandpa so much. I am glad we shall see you soon.

Closing and Signature → Love,
Connor

P.S. I won the snowball fight!   ← Post Script

The Envelope

The return address provides the postal service with a way to get the letter back to you if they cannot deliver it to the person or address you sent it to. The placement of the return and mailing addresses is mportant, since the postal service uses machines to read these. If the machine cannot read it properly, your letter will have to be hand-sorted, which delays delivery.

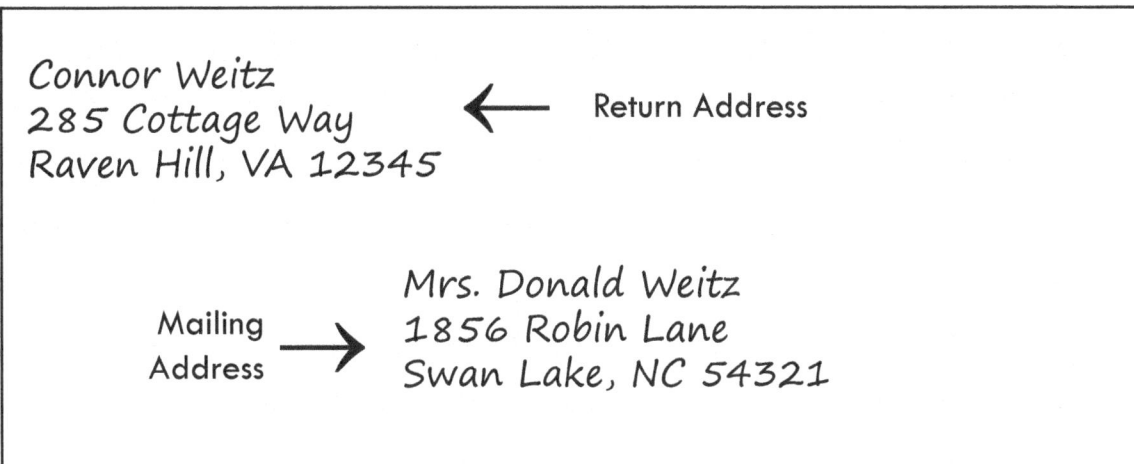

UNITED STATES POSTAL ABBREVIATIONS

These two letter postal abbreviations are recognized by the United States Postal Service. They are written with two capital letters and no end punctuation.

Alabama	AL	Louisiana	LA	Ohio	OH
Alaska	AK	Maine	ME	Oklahoma	OK
Arizona	AZ	Maryland	MD	Oregon	OR
Arkansas	AR	Massachusetts	MA	Pennsylvania	PA
California	CA	Michigan	MI	Rhode Island	RI
Colorado	CO	Minnesota	MN	South Carolina	SC
Connecticut	CT	Mississippi	MS	South Dakota	SD
Delaware	DE	Missouri	MO	Tennessee	TN
Florida	FL	Montana	MT	Texas	TX
Georgia	GA	Nebraska	NE	Utah	UT
Hawaii	HI	Nevada	NV	Vermont	VT
Idaho	ID	New Hampshire	NH	Virginia	VA
Illinois	IL	New Jersey	NJ	Washington	WA
Indiana	IN	New Mexico	NM	West Virginia	WV
Iowa	IA	New York	NY	Wisconsin	WI
Kansas	KS	North Carolina	NC	Wyoming	WY
Kentucky	KY	North Dakota	ND		

District of Columbia   DC

The Business Letter

A business letter has the same basic parts as a friendly letter, but there are a few differences, as you can see below. The name and address of the business are included above the salutation. If you know the name of the person to whom you are writing, that should be included above the business name.

A business letter has a more formal salutation and closing. If you know the name of the person to whom you are addressing the letter, the salutation should be Dear followed by his or her title (Dr., Mr., Mrs., etc.) and last name. If you do not know the specific person to whom your letter should be addressed, use Dear Sir or Madam, followed by a comma. For the closing, use Sincerely or Regards.

Heading →
285 Cottage Way
Raven Hill, Virginia 12345
February 10, 2014

National Air and Space Museum
682 Independence Avenue, SW
Washington, D.C. 20560

← Business Name and Address

Dear Sir or Madam,   ← Greeting (Salutation)

    I am a student at Providence Prep Academy. Our class is studying the night sky. We would like to tour the Albert Einstein Planetarium next month. Please send information on tours and prices, along with dates available for tours in February. We look forward to our visit.

Body ↗

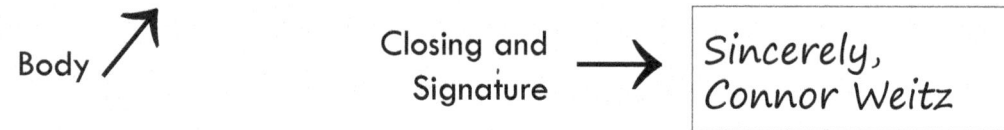

Closing and Signature →
Sincerely,
Connor Weitz

Drawing Page

Drawing Page